GET THE SCOOP of Animal BLOOD!

From Great White Sharks to Blood-Squirting Lizards, 251 Cool Facts

Dawn Cusick

MoonDance

Brimming with creative inspiration, how-to projects, and useful information to enrich your everyday life, Quarto Knows is a favorite destination for those pursuing their interests and passions. Visit our site and dig deeper with our books into your area of interest: Quarto Creates, Quarto Cooks, Quarto Homes, Quarto Lives, Quarto Drives, Quarto Explores, Quarto Gifts, or Quarto Kids.

First Published in 2017 by MoonDance Press, an imprint of The Quarto Group.
6 Orchard Road, Suite 100, Lake Forest, CA 92630, USA.
T (949) 380-7510 **F** (949) 380-7575 **www.QuartoKnows.com**

MoonDance Press titles are also available at discount for retail, wholesale, promotional, and bulk purchase. For details, contact the Special Sales Manager by email at specialsales@quarto.com or by mail at The Quarto Group, Attn: Special Sales Manager, 401 Second Avenue North, Suite 310, Minneapolis, MN 55401 USA.

ISBN: 978-1-63322-227-4

Produced by EarlyLight Books
Design: Celia Naranjo
Cover Image: Ramon Carretero
Page Layout & Image Research: Dawn Cusick
Proofreading: Nicole Sipe

Printed in China
10 9 8 7 6 5 4 3 2 1

CONTENTS

INTRODUCTION 4 & 5

INTRODUCTION

WELCOME to a world of Animal Blood!

You may have noticed that people have some wild responses to blood. Some get squeamish and turn their heads. Others hear the word blood and think about vampires and zombies. Some people pass out. Others just say, "Cool."

If blood makes you squeamish, don't worry. You won't see much blood in this book. If blood makes you pass out, read this book in bed so you won't have far to fall. If blood makes you say "Cool," you're in for a real treat.

Like most things in nature that seem gross when you first hear about them, blood gets more interesting as you learn more. Why do walruses and whales have extra blood? How do some insects and snakes use blood to defend themselves? How do most animals use blood to warm and cool their bodies? How do hibernating animals make it through long winters?

Blood is important to you, too. Whether you're playing a video game, taking a math test, or reading a book, your brain needs lots of energy. To make that energy, your brain cells need lots of oxygen-rich blood. Muscles need lots of energy, too, and they use extra blood vessels to keep them well supplied with oxygen-rich blood.

Have fun getting
The Scoop on Animal Blood!

BLOOD 101

If you think blood is just a red liquid that carries oxygen, you are in for some surprises. Blood helps animals in many ways, and it comes in lots of colors.

Lots of Jobs!

Blood moves oxygen and carbon dioxide gases through animals. It does other important work, too. Blood helps animals keep their bodies the right temperature. It also brings nutrients and hormones to different parts of animal bodies. Blood takes away waste and helps fight disease, too.

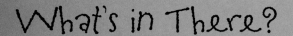

What's in There?

The liquid part of blood is called plasma. About 90 percent of plasma is water. Blood cells move through this liquid. Sugars, salts, wastes, and other molecules move through plasma, too.

More Water, Please

Because there's so much water in plasma, animals need a lot of it. When you don't get enough water, your body tightens its blood vessels, making your heart work harder. These tight blood vessels can cause headaches in some people. If it's hot outside, you can also get heat exhaustion or heat stroke. Wild animals can suffer from these problems, too.

Size It up!

In most land animals, about 7 percent of their body weight is blood. For deep-diving mammals, up to 20 percent of their bodies can be blood. How much do you weigh? Multiply that number by .07 to find out how much your blood weighs!

BLOOD 101

Ready for Work

As blood cells grow, they become different from each other. Some cells will carry oxygen. In vertebrate animals, these cells are red because of a protein called hemoglobin that has iron in it. Others grow into white blood cells that will fight infections. A third type grows into platelets that will help form clots.

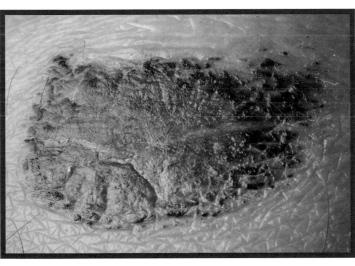

Scabs!

How many scabs have you had in your life? The next time you get one, think about how scabs are made. Scabs begin with lots of platelets that block blood from leaving the body. Vitamins and proteins hold the platelets in place to form a scab.

Recycle!

When blood cells get too old, the liver and the spleen pull them out of circulation. The hemoglobin is sent back to the bones to make new blood cells.

Built-in Bandages

Platelets are much smaller than red and white blood cells. They have special chemicals that help blood clot. They also attach to cuts or tears in blood vessels.

BLOOD 101

To do its work, animal blood must be just the right pH with just the right amount of salts and other chemicals in it. Animals use many cool adaptations to clean and maintain their blood.

Keep It Neutral

Animal blood needs to stay at just the right pH value or the animal will die. Painted turtles can use ions from their shells to change their blood's pH.

Moving Salt

Sharks, skates, and rays use glands in their rectums to remove extra salt from their blood. Saltwater crocodiles use glands on their tongues. When marine turtles move blood through their eyes, it can look like they're crying!

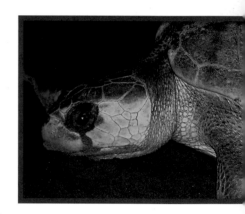

Bird Brains

Birds that feed on marine animals need to get rid of salt, too. They have salt glands in their nostrils. Albatross birds can even drink ocean water. They use glands over their eyes to remove extra salt.

Sneezing Salt

Marine iguanas feed on salty algae from the sea. This diet adds more salt to their blood than their kidneys can remove. To get rid of extra salt, iguanas snort or sneeze it out through their nostrils. Some other lizards can remove salt this way, too.

BLOOD COLORS

Green Blood?

Green-blooded skinks from Papua New Guinea live up to their name: they have green blood! A special protein makes their blood, bones, and tissues green. Check out the green color in the mouth of the green-blooded skink above.

Yellow, Pink, Green

Insects take the prize for the most blood colors. Their clear blood can take on colors from the foods they eat. Sea cucumbers and some other animals have yellow blood.

Purple & Blue, It's True!

Blood cells in spiders, crabs, lobsters, squids, octopuses, and some other animals use copper instead of iron to hold oxygen. The copper causes their blood to come in shades of blue!

Seeing Red

Mosquitos and other blood-sucking insects may look like they have red blood when they're squashed. The red is coming from their host's blood, though, and not their own. Some flies and beetles can look like they have red blood, too. These red colors come from red pigments in their eyes or exoskeletons, and not from their blood.

Pink Blood

Flamingos feed on algae, snails, shrimp, and crabs. When pink pigments in these foods move into flamingo blood, the color travels through their bodies and into their feathers. Biologists have even found the pink color in flamingo eggs!

RED BLOOD CELLS

Red blood cells, called RBCs for short, do important work in vertebrate animals: They carry oxygen. Their membranes are usually very thin, which helps oxygen move inside faster.

Amphibians Take the Prize

Amphibians have oval red blood cells that are larger than fish, reptile, bird, and mammal RBCs. Amphibians may need these large cells because they have very small lungs. Salamanders have larger blood cells than frogs, and more of them.

Bird Blood

Red blood cells in birds are oval shaped. Reptiles have oval red blood cells, too.

Fish!

Red blood cells in fish are also oval. They come in many sizes, depending on the type of fish. How do people know this? In the 1960s, a biologist named Dorothy Chapman Saunders measured red blood cells from more than eight hundred fish in the Red Sea and Puerto Rico. Sounds like a fun job!

Rays & Sharks

Rays and sharks have oval-shaped red blood cells, too, but theirs are a little larger than the cells of their bony fish relatives.

RED BLOOD CELLS

No Nucleus Here

In mammals, red blood cells purge their nucleus as they mature, which helps them carry more oxygen. This sounds like a perfect adaptation, right? It's actually not so perfect. Without a nucleus, there's no DNA. Without DNA, the genes that fix damaged cells cannot be turned on and damaged blood cells must be destroyed. In each of the cells on this page, the white area in the middle is where the nucleus used to be. Most mammals have round RBCs.

Small & Oval

Camel blood cells are smaller than RBCs in most other mammals. Their red blood cells are also oval shaped, instead of round. During droughts, camels drink less water and their blood gets thicker. The smaller size and oval shape help the cells move through thicker blood.

Extra-Large for Me, Please

Walruses and many other diving animals have extra large blood cells to help them hold more oxygen while they are underwater.

BLOOD CELL VENOM

Toxins that affect red blood cells are called hemotoxins. (The prefix hemo comes from the Greek and means blood.) Hemotoxins work by breaking open the membranes around red blood cells. Venoms with strong hemotoxins can cause prey animals to bleed to death from the inside.

Snake Science

Two big groups of snakes, the true vipers and the pit vipers, use hemotoxins to subdue and digest their prey. Although this venom can be deadly, antivenins can save people if they can get to a hospital. The two snakes shown here include a Sumatran pit viper (above) and a temple viper (below).

Bite Sites

Why does skin turn black after some snake and spider bites? The skin dies because venom destroyed red blood cells near the bite. Without oxygen, skin cells die. Bite sites often get big blisters, too.

BLOOD CELL VENOM

Spider Bites

Brown recluse spiders use hemotoxic venom to prey on small insects and other spiders. They don't prey on people, but sometimes they live with them. These spiders may bite people to defend themselves when we surprise them. Brown recluse venom does not kill people, but it can hurt a lot and leave scars.

Cute Face, Bad Bites

The venom in Taipan snakes causes blood to clot, which can block veins and arteries. Bite victims can die in less than an hour if they do not get an antivenin shot. To make antivenins, venomous snakes are milked (left).

Dragon Venom

Komodo dragons use their strong venom to lower their prey's blood pressure, sending them into shock. Dragons feed on large animals such as water buffalo, deer, and other dragons.

MOVING BLOOD

Many animals move blood through their bodies in tubes called vessels. Vertebrates and a few invertebrates use closed circulatory systems, which means the tubes connect with each other.

Thick, Stretchy Tubes

Arteries move blood away from the heart. Arteries are thicker than veins because they are lined with muscles. These muscles let artery tubes open wider (dilate) or squeeze tighter (constrict).

ARTERY

VEIN

Thin Tubes

Veins bring blood to the heart. These large tubes are thinner than arteries and not as stretchy. Most animal veins have valves that stop blood from going in the wrong direction.

Pooling Tubes

When animals rest, about two-thirds of their blood pools in their veins. This is true when you're sitting at your desk in school, too. The next time you need a study break, think about the blood that's pooled in your veins. Get that blood moving with some exercise!

MOVING BLOOD

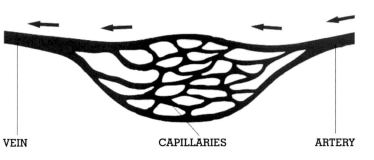

Capillary Beds

Groups of capillaries are called beds. Large muscles that need more oxygen have more capillary beds. The body fat used by hibernating and migrating animals has more capillary beds, too.

VEIN   CAPILLARIES   ARTERY

Open Systems

Octopuses, snails, and insects use open systems to move blood. They do have veins and arteries, but these tubes do not connect with each other. Instead, their vessels empty into their body cavities, where tissues absorb oxygen and release carbon dioxide.

Connecting Tubes

Thin, tiny tubes called capillaries bring oxygen-rich blood from arteries to cells around the body. Capillaries also move carbon dioxide to veins.

Stretch 'Em Out

If you stretched out all of the capillaries in an animal and lined them up, they would be tens of thousands of miles long. In large animals, the distance could be *hundreds* of thousands of miles. Yowza.

BLOOD PRESSURE

Blood pressure is the amount of force moving blood through an animal's body. Check out these cool blood pressure adaptations!

Long Travels

Long legs and necks help giraffes compete with other large herbivores for food. These adaptations cause some blood pressure problems, though. Their large leg veins must move blood from the bottoms of their feet all the way up to their hearts, about six feet (2 m). Their strong leg muscles help move blood against gravity by squeezing their leg veins against nearby bones. Giraffe veins are thicker than veins in many other animals, too. Giraffes have the highest blood pressure in the animal kingdom. It's more than twice as high as a healthy human's blood pressure!

Anti-Gravity Suits

Giraffes are not astronauts and they do not live in outer space. Like astronauts, though, giraffes wear anti-gravity suits that prevent blood from pooling in their legs. Giraffe "suits" are made from a tight, thick skin layer.

High Pressure

Ostriches and emus have higher blood pressures than other birds. Their bodies need this extra pressure to move blood up their necks, against gravity, to their brains.

Predator Pressure

Dragonfly larvae are fierce predators that live in water. To feed, they squeeze their abdomens, which forces blood into their lower lips, helping them grab prey.

BLOOD PRESSURE

Walking Pressure

Just like vertebrate animals, spiders use muscles to move their legs in toward their bodies. Spiders don't have muscles to extend their legs outward, though. Instead, their bodies force blood into their legs to make them move.

Don't believe it? Compare a dead spider to a dead insect. A dead spider will always have its legs tucked in. Why? Because the spider's blood stops moving into its legs once its heart stops beating, making the legs pull inward.

Stop, Wiggle & Roll

Climbing tree snakes often stop on their way up a tree and wiggle their bodies. Why? When tree snakes climb, gravity causes blood to pool in their tails. When tree snakes stop to wiggle, they are really squeezing muscles around their veins, which pushes blood back up to their hearts.

Jumping Pressure

A jumping spider's body can force enough blood into its back legs to let it jump fifty times its body height. That's a lot of blood pressure!

Pressure Cleaning

Reptiles have a sac near their eyes that can fill with blood. When the sac's blood pressure gets high enough, it forces dirt to the corners of the animals' eyes. Who needs washcloths and soap?

Swimming Snakes

Sea snakes do not have the same gravity problems that ground and tree snakes do. Their hearts are in the middle of their bodies because it takes the same force to move blood to their brains as it does to move blood to their tails.

PUMPING BLOOD

The heart is a strong muscle that moves blood when it contracts. Not all animal hearts are the same!

Four Chambers

Mammals and birds have four chambers in their hearts: two atria at the top and two ventricles below. Having two ventricles helps keep oxygen-rich blood away from oxygen-poor blood.

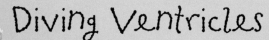

Diving Ventricles

Crocodiles, alligators, and their close relatives have four-chambered hearts, too. These animals also have a flap between their ventricles that lets them send oxygen-poor blood back through their bodies. Why would they do this? Experiments show they may be using the extra carbon dioxide in their blood to make more stomach acid for digesting food. These reptiles can also close off one of their ventricles when they dive to save oxygen.

Three for Me

Octopuses have three hearts! Two hearts bring blood to their gills. A third, larger heart brings blood to the rest of their body. Although octopuses can swim fast when they need to, their third heart stops beating when they swim. Octopuses often crawl to save energy.

PUMPING BLOOD

Three Chambers!

Amphibians and reptiles such as snakes, turtles, and lizards have three chambers in their hearts: one ventricle and two atria. In the ventricle, blood that's carrying oxygen mixes with some blood that has no oxygen.

Two Chambers!

Fish have two-chambered hearts with one atrium and one ventricle. They also have special chambers next to each atrium and ventricle for holding blood. As blood fills the chamber next to the atrium, it tells the heart muscles to contract. As blood fills the chamber next to the ventricle, the pressure goes down, which protects the thin blood vessels in their gills.

Bug Off

Insects use a long vessel along their backs to move blood through their open circulatory systems. Some insects have heart-like chambers in this vessel. Houseflies have three chambers, while cockroaches have thirteen! Insects also have small pumps near their leg joints to push blood into their limbs. Flying insects have extra pumps near their wings.

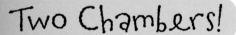

Arches, Instead

Earthworms use five pairs of arches to pump blood through their vessels.

PUMPING BLOOD

Many animals have cool adaptations to their hearts that help their hearts move blood.

Bird Hearts

Birds have large hearts compared to other animals their size. Smaller birds have larger hearts. Hummingbirds take the prize for the largest bird heart for their size. Bird hearts are strong, too. They can pump more blood with every beat than most mammal hearts.

Sloth Hearts

Compared to other animals their size, sloth hearts are small. Sloth hearts also tilt sideways when they hang upside down because their diaphragms push on their hearts.

Bat Hearts

Bats have large hearts for their small size. Their hearts beat more than six hundred times every minute! Bats have extra capillary beds, too. It takes a lot of oxygen to make enough energy to fly!

Tree Snakes

Snakes that live in trees have smaller hearts. Their hearts are also closer to their heads than their ground-living relatives. Biologists believe their heart positions may help the snakes get blood to their brains more easily when they climb trees.

PUMPING BLOOD

The number of times your heart beats in one minute (BPM) is your pulse rate. Each time a heart beats, it forces blood through an animal's body. What's your pulse rate?

Larger, Smaller, Faster, Slower

Usually, the smaller the animal, the faster its pulse rate. Animals with faster pulse rates tend to have shorter lifespans. An animal's size plays a role in pulse rates, too. Confused? Compare the average pulse rates and lifespans of the animals below. Remember, these are just averages. Many animals live longer than the average.

Hamster
PULSE: 450 BPM
LIFESPAN: 3 YEARS

Rabbit
PULSE: 205 BPM
LIFESPAN: 9 YEARS

Cat
PULSE: 205 BPM
LIFESPAN: 9 YEARS

Horse
PULSE: 44 BPM
LIFESPAN: 40 YEARS

PUMPING BLOOD

Fight? Flight? Freeze?

When animals sense danger, their brains release a chemical called adrenalin into their bloodstreams. This hormone makes blood vessels tighten, sending more blood to their brains, hearts, and large muscles. Adrenalin also causes the body to release sugar and fat into the blood-stream for extra energy.

Dive, Baby, Dive!

Marine turtles slow down their heart-beats to save oxygen when they dive. These turtles also have extra red blood cells to help them hold more oxygen.

Hearing Heartbeats?

Have you ever heard your pulse in your pillow? When arteries near our ears press against our skulls when we lie down, we may hear our pulsing blood.

Up & Down

When you're sleeping, your body does not need as much blood. Your heart does not work as hard so your pulse rate goes down. When you exercise, your muscles need more oxygen, so your heart pumps faster, making your pulse rate go up.

MOUNTAIN BLOOD

Animals living in the world's high-altitude mountains could have big blood problems. The higher up you go, the less oxygen there is in the air. Adaptations help them survive.

Have a Heart

Yaks (above) and antelopes (right) from Tibet have larger hearts that let them move more blood through their bodies. Their red blood cells can also hold more oxygen than RBCs in most low-altitude animals.

Take a Deep Breath

Mountain-living llamas from South America have four times more red blood cells than humans! Llamas also have large lungs that bring in more oxygen with every breath.

MOUNTAIN BLOOD

Extra, Extra, Read All About It!

Many small mammals from South American mountains, including viscachas (left) and chinchillas (right), have more red blood cells and more hemoglobin than mammals their size living at sea level.

Special Chickens?

Like many other high-altitude animals, Tibetan chickens have more red blood cells and more room on those cells to hold oxygen. Tibet is also home to dog breeds such as this Tibetan terrier with blood adaptations.

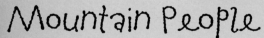

Mountain People

Tibetan people have been living high in the sky for more than 3,000 years. Instead of making more red blood cells, they make fewer. Having fewer red blood cells keeps their blood thinner, which helps their blood move through small capillaries. People from Tibet breathe in and out more often than people from flat lands, letting them take in more oxygen. Their blood vessels also stretch more.

SPACE BLOOD

Doctors and scientists have learned a lot about blood, gravity, and radiation from space travel. Humans and other animals traveling to space receive many blood tests.

Time & Space

Blood doesn't bubble or boil in space, but living in microgravity causes other problems for astronauts. On Earth, gravity pushes blood downward into the legs, and the heart works against gravity to pump it back up. In space, blood pools higher in the body, giving many astronauts puffy faces.

SPACE BLOOD

Welcome Home!

Astronauts return from space with less blood and fewer red blood cells. They may feel dizzy from the blood that's pooled in their heads. If astronauts have been in space for a while, their hearts may have weakened because they didn't need to do the hard work of pumping blood against gravity while in space. Like other muscles, their hearts become stronger after the astronauts spend time back on Earth.

Animals in Space

Monkeys, dogs, and mice were early space pioneers in the 1940s and 1950s. Apes, fish, frogs, lizards, snakes, snails, and spiders have also been part of space experiments. The animals receive blood tests before and after their travels.

Far right, above, and below: Chimpanzees Enos and Ham helped scientists learn how primates handle space travel.

Right and below: A frog and a fish help scientists learn more about microgravity.

MEDICINE BLOOD

Human medicines can come from some wild places! Blood from crocodiles, mice, snakes, and even horseshoe crabs helps keep humans healthy.

Healthy Blood

Biologists have found proteins in crocodile blood that may protect them from diseases caused by some fungi, viruses, and bacteria. After a lot of research, these blood proteins may help make human medicines.

Young Blood

When scientists give blood from younger mice to older mice, the older mice change. Their bodies make new brain and muscle cells. Scientists may be able to use this information to develop drugs for people with brain or muscle damage.

Snake Test

Doctors use venom from Russell's vipers to test people for blood clotting diseases. Doctors don't inject the venom into the patient. Instead, they take a small amount of blood from the patient and mix it with some viper venom, and then watch for blood clots.

Blood Editing

You have probably edited your writing for a teacher, right? You look over your work, find mistakes, and fix them. Some day, scientists may be able to treat blood diseases by editing DNA in young blood cells. Scientists still have a lot to learn, but it's exciting research.

MEDICINE BLOOD

Germ-Fighting Blood

Horseshoe crabs use bacteria-fighting cells in their blood to help them stay healthy. These cells can help people fight infections, too. Doctors use horseshoe crab blood to test human blood for diseases. Doctors also use horseshoe crab blood to make sure there are no bacteria in medical supplies such as pacemakers and dental tools.

Blood Donations

Drug companies remove about 30 percent of each horseshoe crab's blue blood. Then, they return the crabs to the ocean. Scientists are researching ways to make the chemical from the crab's blood in labs so they will not need donations from living crabs anymore.

BRAIN BLOOD

Animals need a good, clean blood supply to their brains to stay healthy. They also need the blood to be just the right temperature—not too cold and not too hot.

Talking Blood

When a person has a stroke, the blood supply to his or her brain can be affected. Without blood, brain cells can die from lack of oxygen. If a stroke happens in the brain's language center, the person may lose his or her speech. If a stroke happens in the brain's memory center, the person may not be able to remember his or her past.

Brrrrr

Ever wonder why frozen drinks and ice cream can make your head hurt? Scientists wondered, too, so they studied brain scans of people with brain freeze. The scans showed extra blood rushing into an artery in their brains. This extra blood may create extra pressure, causing the pain people call brain freeze. Why would the body suddenly send extra blood to the brain? To warm it up!

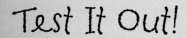

Test It Out!

For the sake of science, you should do some experiments with ice cream and frozen drinks. First, see if you can cause brain freeze by letting a frozen treat rest against the roof of your mouth. If it causes brain freeze, try to stop the pain with a drink of warm water. Wait a few minutes and then have another bite or sip of your frozen treat. This time, try to keep the treat away from the roof of your mouth. Did you still get brain freeze?

BRAIN BLOOD

No Trespassing

All animals with backbones have special cells that protect their brains by forming the blood brain barrier (BBB). The BBB works to keep bacteria and other microbes from moving through blood to the brain.

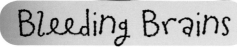

Bleeding Brains

One kind of flesh-eating amoeba gets around the blood brain barrier by moving through nasal sinuses. These amoebas usually eat bacteria, but since the BBB keeps bacteria out, the amoebas eat brain tissue instead, causing it to bleed. Luckily, it's hard for amoebas to move up human noses so this disease is rare.

Fainting Brains

When an animal's brain does not get enough blood, fainting is a quick fix. Think about it: Once you go from standing to lying down, your heart doesn't have to pump blood upward, against gravity.

You may have heard about fainting goats. These animals stiffen and fall over when they are afraid or startled. Despite their funny name, there is nothing wrong with the blood in their brain and they are not really fainting.

Mad Cows

When small proteins called prions cross the blood brain barrier, they cause mad cow disease in cattle.

Nerve Cells

Crayfish can turn some of their blood cells into nerve cells in their brains. *Wow!*

THERMOSTAT BLOOD

Many animals use their blood and blood vessels to keep their bodies at just the right temperature. How many of these adaptations do you think people use?

Warm Stripes, Cool Stripes

Stripes may help zebras cool themselves in hot habitats. Dark stripes have more blood vessels under them than light stripes. This difference may help zebras stay cool by giving them a way to release heat. Zebra biologists have found that zebras from hotter places have more stripes than zebras from cooler places.

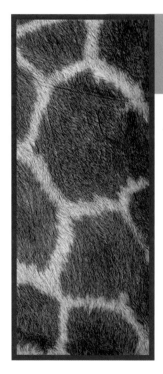

Warm Spots, Cool Spots

When biologists measured the temperatures of giraffe fur, they found that darker spots have more blood vessels under them than lighter spots. The extra blood vessels help giraffes cool off.

Snow Shoes

How can cold-weather birds stand on snow and ice without their feet freezing to the ground? Birds such as these penguins have fewer blood vessels in their lower legs, letting them keep the temperature of their feet colder than the temperature of the rest of their body. The birds also constrict their blood vessels in cold weather, and expand them in warmer weather.

THERMOSTAT BLOOD

Shivering Blood

Warm-blooded animals can shiver to warm their bodies. Shivering happens when groups of muscles quickly contract. The muscle contractions create heat, which warms their blood. Shivering also moves blood closer to internal organs.

Shivering Snakes

Like other reptiles, pythons are cold blooded. Females may coil their bodies around their eggs and shiver to warm them.

Blood Heat

It's easier for animals to lose body heat in water than on land, and many aquatic mammals have special adaptations to help them stay warm. In the tails of dolphins and some other whales, veins wrap around arteries, which moves extra heat from their muscles through their bodies.

COOLING BLOOD

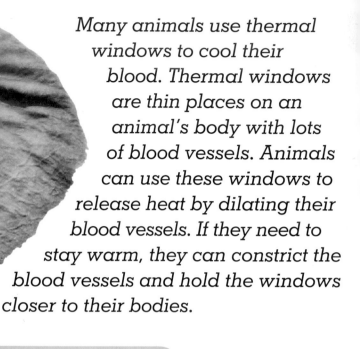

Many animals use thermal windows to cool their blood. Thermal windows are thin places on an animal's body with lots of blood vessels. Animals can use these windows to release heat by dilating their blood vessels. If they need to stay warm, they can constrict the blood vessels and hold the windows closer to their bodies.

Heat Release

Many desert animals use their extra-large ears as thermal windows. As heat leaves through their ears, their bodies cool down. A desert fox is shown here.

Flapping Blood

At first sight, an elephant's large ears may look like giant fans. Elephants don't flap their ears to cool their faces, though. Instead, they are cooling their blood! An elephant's ears are very thin, with lots of large blood vessels. When it's hot, elephants dilate these blood vessels so heat can leave their bodies. Elephants that live in hotter places have larger ears. Don't believe it? Compare the ear sizes of African and Indian elephants. Now look up the average temperatures of their habitats.

COOLING BLOOD

Cool Me Off!

Animals such as African buffaloes (right) and ibex goats use their horns as thermal windows to cool their blood.

Tall birds such as this African stork can dilate the blood vessels in their legs to cool off. When birds release heat this way, their legs can be more than 10 degrees F (12 C) hotter than the rest of their bodies. Now that's a thermal window!

Tails Up

Squirrels use large blood vessels on the undersides of their tails as thermal windows to help them cool off.

Think Pink

Arctic walruses dilate blood vessels in their upper bodies to cool off, which makes their skin look pink. When the walruses are cold, the blood vessels tighten, which makes their skin look brown.

COOLING BLOOD

Panting Blood

Foxes, pigs, and many other mammals pant when they are hot. As air moves over their tongues, their blood cools off. Birds pant, too!

Breathe Through Your Nose?

Many mammals cool the blood traveling to their brains by letting warm blood from their hearts pass over blood that has been cooled by their noses. How do noses cool blood? When animals breathe in and out through their moist nostrils, the vessels near that skin are exposed to air that is cooler than their body temperature, which cools nearby blood!

Cooling Blood

Black vultures and turkey vultures cool their blood by a funny way. They pee on their legs! As the urine evaporates, it cools their legs and the blood inside them. Storks and condors cool their blood this way, too.

COOLING BLOOD

Fluttering Blood

Some birds vibrate the loose skin under their necks to move hot air over their tongues. This kind of heat release is called fluttering. Different birds flutter at different speeds. Biologists counted more than two hundred flutters per minute in brown pelicans and horned owls! Impressed? Cormorants and doves flutter more than seven hundred times per minute!

Run for Your Life

When prey animals run from predators, the extra heat from their hard-working muscles heats their blood. Nose breathing is extra important for these animals because hot blood can damage their brains.

WARMING BLOOD

Amphibians, reptiles, and fish warm their bodies with heat from the sun and water. Body heat is important because warm muscles and organs work faster than cold ones.

Hitchhiking Heat

Have you ever seen reptiles resting next to each other in large groups? They don't stay near each other because they are close friends. Instead, they have chosen the same sunny place to warm their bodies. Basking together on this page are painted turtles (right) and bearded dragons (below). Basking alligators are on the facing page (bottom).

WARMING BLOOD

Weather Changes

Many fish make fewer red blood cells in the winter, which makes their blood thinner and easier to move through their bodies. When temperatures rise in the spring, fish such as this trout start making more red blood cells.

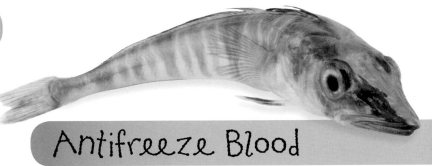

Antifreeze Blood

Some Antarctic fish have a special protein in their blood that keeps the blood from freezing. Many icefish also have clear blood because their bodies do not make red blood cells. These fish can live without red blood cells because they have a lot of blood vessels near their skin's surface and very few scales. The cold waters they live in have so much dissolved oxygen that the fish get oxygen through their gills *and* through their skin!

WARMING BLOOD

Warm-Blooded Fish?

What? A warm-blooded fish? Biologists were surprised, too! Opah fish live in cold, deep waters. Being warm blooded makes them better predators because they can swim faster and see better. They also don't need to swim toward the surface to warm their bodies, as many other deepwater predators do.

Science at Work

When biologists noticed unusual blood vessel nets around opah gills, they wondered if these vessels could be warming the fishes' blood. To test their idea, biologists tagged fishes with sensors that measured the temperatures of their bodies and the water around them.

WARMING BLOOD

Warm-Blooded Parts

Mako and great white sharks use wonderful nets to give their muscles extra heat, which helps them swim in fast bursts when needed. Tunas can use wonderful nets this way, too. Sailfish, marlins, and swordfish have wonderful nets near their eyes and brains, which helps them see prey. The phrase "wonderful nets" comes from the Latin words *retia mirabilia*.

Opah Nets

Opah fish keep their bodies warm in a different way than other warm-blooded animals. A large web of arteries and veins surrounds their gills. Warm blood in their veins heats up cold blood from their arteries because the vessels are so close to each other, keeping the fishes' bodies about 9 degrees F (5 degrees C) warmer than the water around them.

In case you were wondering . . . Like other fish, the blood in the opah's veins is warm because of the heat from their muscles. The blood in arteries near their gills is very cold because of the cold water around them.

Nursery Heat

Some wasps warm their eggs and pupae with hot air heated by their blood.

DIVING BLOOD

Animals use some cool adaptations to live and feed in deepwater habitats. Without extra oxygen from these adaptations, they would not have enough energy to find food and escape from predators.

Wow!

Elephant seals can dive almost a mile (1.6 km) under water and stay under for two hours. Even more amazing, they only need to breathe at the surface for a few minutes before they can dive again. How do they do it? Extra-large blood cells and extra blood help. They also have special places in their abdomens called sinuses where their bodies can hold more oxygen-rich blood.

Diving for Dinner

Walruses use extra-large blood cells to help them dive deep. Their bodies also have more blood than other animals their size. Don't believe it? Do you remember that about 7 percent of a human's body weight comes from blood? For walruses, that number is about 12 percent!

DIVING BLOOD

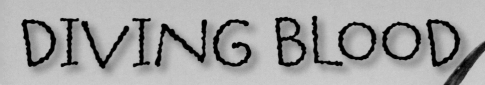

Deep-Diving Birds

Emperor penguins dive more than 1,600 feet (more than 500 meters) to find food. They can stay under water for more than 20 minutes. Like some other cold-water diving animals, emperor penguins move their blood away from their skin to help them stay warm.

Mini Oxygen Tanks?

A protein called myoglobin holds extra oxygen in the muscles of mammals. Some diving animals have thirty times more oxygen-holding myoglobin than land mammals!

Bubble Blood

When people dive under water with SCUBA gear, they must return to the surface slowly. If they resurface too quickly, they can get bubbles in their blood from nitrogen gas, which can make them very sick. This disease is called "the bends" because people with it often bend over in pain.

DIVING BLOOD

50 Gallons, 190 Liters?

The hearts of blue whales can pump more than 50 gallons (190 L) of blood through their bodies with every beat. That's a lot of blood! During deep dives, their hearts slow down, and most of their blood stays in their brains and hearts.

DIVING BLOOD

Whales Do It. Why Can't We?

Whales can swim to the surface at high speeds without getting the bends. When whales dive deeper than 100 feet (30.5 m), they collapse their lungs to keep nitrogen out of their blood.

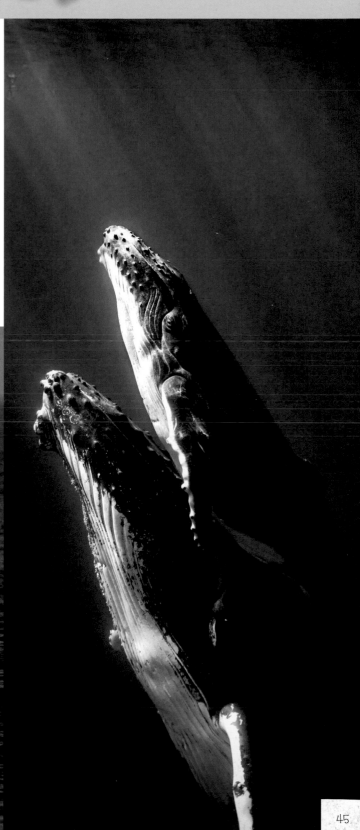

HIBERNATING BLOOD

When animals hibernate, their bodies change in many ways. Their blood spends less time near their skin and more time near their organs. Their blood also becomes thicker.

Slow Down!

Hibernating hearts slow way down. A flying bat's heart can go from more than six hundred beats per minute to less than forty when it's hibernating! A woodchuck's heartbeat drops from eighty beats a minute to four. An Arctic squirrel's pulse drops from several hundred beats per minute to just one or two!

More Red, Fewer White

Many hibernating animals have more red blood cells, which lets them take in more oxygen from each breath. Most hibernating animals have fewer white blood cells during hibernation. Having fewer white blood cells makes room for the extra red blood cells, which is a good adaptation. The adaptation isn't perfect, though, because hibernating animals are more likely to catch infections.

HIBERNATING BLOOD

Sweet Blood

Wood frogs from Alaska and Canada can hibernate in very cold forests, as low as -80 degrees F (-62 C) in the winter. How can they do this? Why doesn't their blood freeze? Why don't ice crystals cut through their veins and arteries? So many cool questions! When it's time to hibernate, their livers release lots of sugar. The sugar mixes with water in their cells, forming a thick syrup that doesn't freeze. Their hearts also stop beating during hibernation!

No Blood Clots Here

When people spend too much time sitting still or lying down, platelets can clump together and form clots. Hibernating animals can spend months without moving and never get blood clots. Why? Their blood does not have platelets!

Hibernating Shots?

Biologists have found a chemical that may save human lives in blood from hibernating squirrels. When they inject the chemical into squirrels that are wide awake, the squirrels start hibernating. When people lose a lot of blood after an accident, their body tissues can die from lack of oxygen. A hibernation shot could keep their bodies safe until they get care.

SMELLING BLOOD

Many animals are very aware of nearby blood odors. Some animals use those smells to find food. Other animals use the smells as alarms, warning them of nearby predators.

Spiny Lobster Blood

Spiny lobsters feed at night, when there isn't much light. Because it's so dark, they can't use their vision to see predators. When a predator feeds on a nearby lobster, chemicals in the lobster's blood escape into the water, warning other lobsters that danger is near. Because lobsters do not have noses, how do they smell blood? With their antennae, of course!

Test It Out

How do biologists know the alarm cues are coming from the spiny lobster's blood and not from mucus or somewhere else? With experiments! Biologists kept large aquarium tanks filled with spiny lobsters in their lab. When biologists added small amounts of blood to the tanks, almost all of the lobsters moved away from the blood and tried to hide.

SMELLING BLOOD

Sharks & Blood

Have you heard that sharks can smell one drop of blood from anywhere in the ocean? Sharks do have a strong sense of smell, but they can only smell a drop of blood in an Olympic-sized swimming pool, not in the entire ocean.

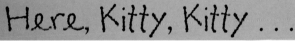

Here, Kitty, Kitty . . .

Have you ever smelled blood? Biologists wondered what causes its metallic smell. After many experiments, they found the chemical that causes the smell. When biologists placed the chemical on logs at a wildlife park, Siberian tigers licked, bit, and pawed at the logs.

Look Out!

Some vertebrate animals use blood as alarm cues. These animals include some fish, rats, chickens, and even cows. The blood tells the animals that a predator may be nearby, and animals quickly move away from the blood source after smelling it. Some prey animals also stop searching for food for a while after smelling blood.

DEFENDING BLOOD

Some animals can release some of their blood to scare or injure predators. This adaptation is called reflex bleeding. What's a little blood when your life's at stake?

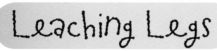

Leaching Legs

There are more than five thousand species of ladybugs (also called ladybirds and lady beetles) living around the world. Adult ladybugs can release toxic blood from their leg joints to repel predators. If you pick one up, be gentle!

Multiply by Four!

How tall are you? Multiply your height by four. Now multiply your height by five. Armored ground crickets can squirt their blood four to five times their body height! They also save toxic blood on the top side of their bodies and use it to scare away lizards and other predators reaching down to bite them.

Bloody-Nosed Beetles

These insects ooze a bad-tasting blood when threatened. Since they cannot fly, this defense may protect them from bird predators. Bloody-nosed beetles have red blood, which explains their funny name.

DEFENDING BLOOD

Lightning Blood

Some fireflies release blood filled with bad-tasting toxins from their front wings and just below their heads. When biologists offered the fireflies to spider predators, the spiders picked up the fireflies, but quickly dropped them!

Take That!

It's not just adult insects that can reflex bleed. Some larvae can do it, too. Sawfly larvae squirt a blue-green liquid to protect themselves from wasps and ants.

Popping Blood

At least two kinds of stoneflies use reflex bleeding to surprise or delay predators. One stonefly species can spray its yellow-orange blood for up to ten inches (25 cm). Another species has blood that thickens when the blood hits its target. Biologists have watched ants trying to remove thick blobs of blood from their faces. As the ants worked to remove the blobs, the blood thickened even more!

Blister Beetles

If a blister beetle reflex bleeds on you, guess what happens? Toxins in their blood cause burns and blisters on animal skin. One chemical in their blood is so strong that it's used in human medicines to remove warts.

Sick Bleeders

At least one kind of caterpillar reflex bleeds when it has a virus or when it's disturbed. Sometimes, these caterpillars suck some of the blood back into their bodies through their spines!

DEFENDING BLOOD

Some reptiles use reflex bleeding to protect themselves from predators. Changes to the blood pressure adaptations that help them clean their eyes let them release some blood without bleeding to death.

Back off!

Some species of short-horned lizards can squirt blood from sacs near their eyes up to six feet away (2 m). *Say whaaaaaat?* The blood spray surprises predators such as coyotes and foxes. The blood also tastes bad because horned lizards feed on venomous harvester ants. Toxins from the ant's venom stay in the lizards' blood.

Give It a Try

To squirt blood, horned lizards squeeze several pairs of muscles near their eyes. The muscles tighten around a vein, increasing its blood pressure and pushing blood out of the lizard's body with force. Try squeezing the muscles around your eyes. People will think you're winking at them!

DEFENDING BLOOD

Boa Bleeding

A dwarf boa from the Caribbean can reflex bleed from its eyes and nose.

Did This Snake Fool You?

The European grass snake plays dead to confuse predators. While pretending, the snake rolls over, holds its mouth open, and oozes blood from its nose and mouth.

NO BLOOD

Although blood is very important to animals, there are times and places where they may not have blood.

Ha, Ha, Fooled 'Ya!

Some animals can confuse predators by breaking off body parts when threatened. This behavior is called reflex amputation. Grasshoppers, katydids, crane flies, walking sticks, and some other insects can leave legs behind, while some lizards can drop their tails.

No Need for Bandages

How can these animals lose body parts without bleeding to death? Animals that use reflex amputation have special places on their bodies called fracture lines. In insects and lobsters, the leg joints near the fracture lines quickly seal up so blood cannot escape. These animals also have low blood pressure. In lizards, the fracture lines are between their tail vertebrae. Some lizards can regrow lost tails.

NO BLOOD

Bye-Bye, Old Skin

When reptiles molt, the cells in the outer skin layer lose their blood supply, causing the skin cells to die. Snakes shed this dead skin all in one piece, while other reptiles shed their skin in pieces. Younger reptiles shed more often than older ones.

No Blood Here

In vertebrate animals, ears, noses, and joints are made from cartilage, which does not have blood vessels in it.

Underwater Tricksters

Lobsters can lose their limbs and their antennae when threatened by predators. Sea cucumbers, sea stars, and brittle stars can also regrow body parts. These animals don't bleed to death because most of their blood is made from seawater. When they need more, they pump it in.

SURPRISING BLOOD

The more you learn about animals, the more you may be surprised by some of the odd places their bodies have blood. When you think about the energy their bodies need to work well, though, it isn't so surprising.

Checking Pulses

Many animals use whiskers to help them sense the world around them. Tigers use their whiskers to help them find a pulse in the necks of their prey. The pulse tells the tigers where to find large blood vessels. The nerve cells that make whiskers work so well have a strong blood supply.

Beware the Quick!

Animals have blood in their claws, too. The area closest to their bodies with blood supply is called the quick. When people trim their pet's nails, they need to avoid the quick. In light-colored nails, you can see the quick. In dogs with darker nails, pet owners need to be extra careful.

SURPRISING BLOOD

O$_2$ for Embryos

Growing embryos need oxygen, too. Look at a chicken egg or its shell under a microscope or a magnifying glass and you can see pores that let oxygen and carbon dioxide in and out. Not impressed? Check out the blood vessels in the membrane of the snake egg to the right.

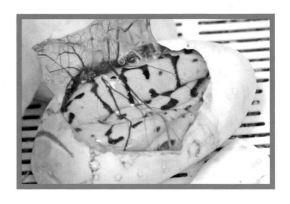

Skin Breathers

Mudskipper fish can spend time on land. They use many small blood vessels close to the surface of their skin and inside their mouths to breathe. Frogs, salamanders, and newts use blood vessels to move oxygen into their bodies this way, too.

Velvet Blood

Every spring, male deer grow new antlers covered with a fuzzy layer called velvet. The velvet layer is filled with blood vessels that bring oxygen and nutrients to the new antlers. When the antlers finish growing, the deer scrape off the velvet layer by rubbing their antlers against bushes and trees.

GLASS BLOOD

Animals with see-through skin are called glass animals. Biologists like working with glass animals because they can study blood vessels and organs in living animals.

Glass Catfish

This see-through fish goes by several names, including ghost fish, phantom fish, and X-ray fish. It lives in streams in Southeast Asia. Check out the blood vessels running from the head to the tail across the top of the fish.

Glass Frogs

Glass frogs live in Central and South America. The undersides of their bodies are see-through, allowing people to view the frogs' hearts, blood vessels, and other organs at work. Some glass frogs are see-through on their top sides, too.

You can see the heart, blood vessels, and a few organs on the undersides of some geckos.

GLASS BLOOD

Meet Casper, the Research Fish

For a long time, scientists who studied blood diseases in people and other animals had to use their imaginations a lot. They could not see blood vessels and blood cells growing and changing. About ten years ago, one group of scientists used genetics to make glass zebrafish. Why zebrafish? These fish have been used to study vertebrate animals for decades so scientists already knew a lot about them.

With glass zebrafish, scientists have learned a lot about how blood cells and vessels work in living animals. Blood cells can be labeled with glowing dyes (above) that let scientists follow them as they age. They can even see blood in developing embryos. This research has helped scientists test ideas and develop new drugs.

Glow!

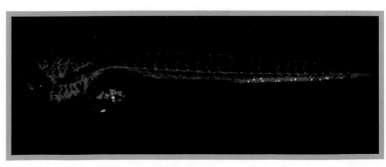

Left and right: Labeled blood cells can be seen in these embryos. Each color shows cells that are a different age.

BLOOD FEEDERS

Blood Helpers

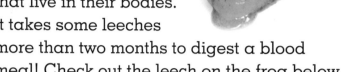

Leeches cannot digest blood by themselves. They need help from two kinds of bacteria that live in their bodies. It takes some leeches more than two months to digest a blood meal! Check out the leech on the frog below.

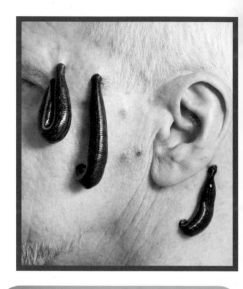

Dr. Leech

Doctors use leeches after some surgeries to keep blood moving. These medical leeches have been raised in labs. Some people believe leeches can clean their bodies, and wear them on their faces, backs, and scalps.

Bite Marks

Leeches with two jaws leave V-shaped bite marks. Leeches with three jaws leave Y-shaped bite marks. Ouch!

BLOOD FEEDERS

Tick Troubles

Ticks feed on blood during three of their life stages: larvae, nymphs, and adults. They live as parasites on mammals, birds, and reptiles, and cause more diseases than any other blood-sucking animal. Like leeches, ticks use heat and carbon dioxide from moving animals to find hosts.

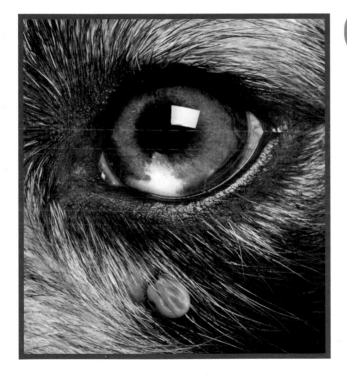

Blood Math

You may have been surprised or grossed out the first time you saw a tick swollen with blood. You may be even more surprised or grossed out to learn that ticks can hold two to six hundred times their body weight in blood. Yowza, that's a lot of blood. There are more than 850 types of ticks in the world.

Female ticks use energy from their blood meals to make eggs.

Vampire Moths

Think quick: What do animal skin and fruit skin have in common? To you and your friends, not much. To a vampire moth, a lot. Vampire moths use needle-sharp mouthparts to feed on blood and fruit juice. Only male moths feed on blood. Biologists are designing experiments to find out why!

BLOOD FEEDERS

There may be more than 900 bat species, but only three types feed on blood. The common vampire bat feeds on mammals and birds. The hairy-legged vampire bat and the white-winged vampire bat feed mostly on birds.

What's a Little Blood?

Vampire bats make small cuts with their teeth and lap the blood with their tongues, the way house cats lap milk. Vampire bats only need about 2 tablespoons (30 mL) of blood per day. Special chemicals in their saliva stop clotting and keep blood vessels from constricting. The bats to the left live in a zoo so their blood meals are brought to them every day.

The Nose Knows

How do vampire bats find blood vessels on animals covered with fur or feathers? Special heat sensors on their noses guide them to places with blood vessels close to the skin.

Fact or Fiction?

In many vampire movies, the stars of the show are large fruit bats, not vampire bats. Why would directors choose to film the wrong bat? Fruit bats are more than thirty-five times larger than vampire bats, making them easier to film and easier to see in finished movies. Can you see blood vessels in this fruit bat's wings?

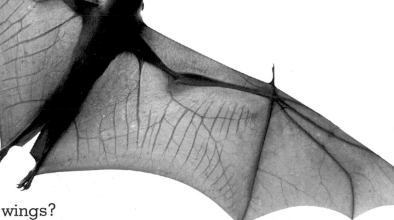

BLOOD FEEDERS

Bye-Bye, Plasma

After a vampire bat feeds, the plasma part of its meal quickly moves across its stomach lining and into its bloodstream. From there, the bat's kidneys remove the extra plasma fluid from its blood, where it leaves the bat's body as urine. Why do vampire bats go to so much work for a blood meal only to pee most of it out? The high-energy part of blood comes from the blood cells. The extra weight from their prey's plasma just makes it harder for them to fly.

BLOOD FEEDERS

Friend or Foe?

Red- and yellow-billed oxpeckers are well known for eating ticks and other parasites on large African mammals. Oxpeckers eat more than parasites, though. Sometimes, they break open scabs or make new wounds on their mammal hosts to get blood meals. When you think about it from a bird's point of view, maybe there's not much difference between feeding on parasites filled with mammal blood and feeding directly on their host's blood.

BLOOD FEEDERS

Patience Pays

Another bird from the Galapagos Islands, the hood mockingbird, breaks open scabs on iguanas and boobies for blood meals. The birds also follow pregnant sea lions, waiting for a chance to get blood from afterbirth. Why do Galapagos mockingbirds feed on blood but mockingbirds from other places do not? Biologists believe it's because there are so few foods available on the remote islands.

Vampire Finches

On Wolf Island in the Galapagos, vampire finches (right) feed on the blood of boobie birds. To feed, the finches use their sharp beaks to break open skin near the boobie's tail feathers. Vampire finches also eat ticks on iguanas and seeds.

BLOOD FEEDERS

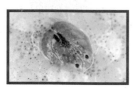

Blood makes a high-energy food for many animals. Some blood feeders break into blood vessels from the outside, while others get blood from inside.

Fish Food

Although fish lice usually do not take enough blood to kill a fish, the wounds they leave on fish skin can cause deadly infections. Some lice feed on blood supplies in the gills, which can make it hard for fish to breathe.

Tongue-Eating Louse

Another type of louse (left) bites into fish tongues. The louse drinks blood from the tongue until it falls off. Then, the louse lives where the tongue used to be, feeding on the fish's blood.

Blood Flukes

Blood flukes live as parasites in the blood of many kinds of animals. Some of these flatworms cause diseases. Others damage body tissues. They feed on their host's blood by biting into veins. Rows of suckers around their mouths help them hang on.

BLOOD FEEDERS

Lamprey Bites

If you saw the top of a lamprey in the ocean, you might think it was a cute little fish. When you saw the lamprey's mouth, though, cute would be the last thing on your mind. You might even shiver. Lampreys have a suction-cup-like mouth that's lined with rows of sharp teeth.

When a lamprey latches onto a fish host, it taps into the fish's capillary beds. The lamprey gets a free ride while it feasts on the host's blood. In one study, biologists found that lampreys can eat almost 30 percent of a fish's blood in a week. Some of the lamprey's hosts die. Others are left with large, circular wounds.

BLOOD FEEDERS

Blood Stealers

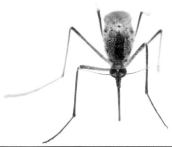

Mosquitos may leave more than itchy bumps when they bite. When mosquitos feed, they can transfer their parasites and viruses from one bite victim to another with some of their blood and saliva. Pets can also get diseases such as heartworms from mosquitos.

BLOOD FEEDERS

Score!

Some animals feed only on blood. Others feed on blood when they're lucky enough to find it. The butter-flies above are sucking fresh blood from a sock.

Greedy Feeders

Lice parasites feed on blood from many kinds of animals. They use special pumps in their throats to move blood into their bodies. Unlike leeches, lice feed on blood every few hours. You can see blood inside the louse above. Lice feces (poop) can be dark red because it has a lot of host blood in it.

Bed Bugs

Bed bugs bite and re-bite until they find a capillary to suck blood from. Like many other blood-feeding insects, young bed bugs must get blood meals before they can molt.

OUUUUUUCHHHH!

Ever wonder why some insect bites hurt more than others? Female deer flies and horse flies do not have needle-like mouthparts for sucking blood. Instead, they use two pairs of blade-like mouthparts to make cuts in skin. When the skin bleeds, they use sponge-like mouthparts to soak up the blood.

BLOOD FEEDERS

Bloody Backs

An insect parasite called the sheep ked feeds on sheep blood. Infected sheep may have reddish-brown stains in their wool, as shown below. The keds are not spilling blood as they feed. Instead, the stains come from blood-rich feces the keds leave behind. Ewww.

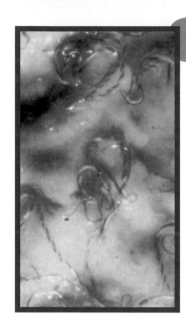

Blood Stripes

Barber pole worms feed on blood from the stomach walls of sheep (left), goats, and other mammals. The animals can die from blood loss if too many of these roundworms feed on them. The red stripes that run down the worms are blood they've taken from their hosts.

BLOOD FEEDERS

Blood Stealers

Jumping spiders and mites can feed on mammal blood without ever biting a mammal. How? They prey on mosquitos that have bulging, red abdomens filled with blood meals! Flies, chiggers, and other ticks feed on tick blood.

Hitchhiking Blood

Female mites live as parasites, feeding on their hosts' blood. The mites need the blood for their eggs to develop. Young mites need blood meals to grow and molt. Many mites live on just one type of host, while others are not so picky. There are dragonfly mites, lizard mites, spider mites, snake mites, mice mites, pigeon mites, and many more.

Honeybee Mites

Mites climb onto bees as they move from flower to flower. When the bees return to their colony, the mites can infect hives, killing hundreds or even thousands of growing larvae.

BLOOD TESTS

Blood tests help doctors and veterinarians learn about their patients in many ways. Usually, they only need to take a small amount of blood for testing.

Blood Groups

Most people have one of four blood groups: A, B, AB, or O. Dogs have eight blood groups, while cats only have three. Cows have eleven blood groups, and horses have more than thirty! Human blood also gets labeled with a plus or a minus that tells doctors whether they have a special protein on their blood cells. Doctors learned about this protein from research with rhesus monkeys. The protein is named after the rhesus monkeys, Rh+ or Rh-.

Hey, Wait, What About Bombay?

A few hundred people in the world belong to the Bombay Blood Group. This blood group came from a mutation in India long ago. People with the mutation can give blood to any other blood group, but can only receive Bombay blood. Only a few blood banks in the world stock this rare blood.

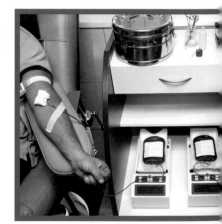

Microscope Tales

Doctors and vets may look at the sizes and shapes of blood cells. They may also look for blood parasites. People who come from places with malaria, for example, may have blood cells with a sickle shape (below) that help fight a blood parasite. Sickle cells cannot carry as much oxygen, and can make people sick.

Transfusion Confusion

Before a doctor or veterinarian can give blood to a patient, they must know the patient's blood group, or type. In the early 1900s, a doctor from Austria learned how to test blood for type. Before then, patients died when they received blood transfusions with the wrong blood type.

BLOOD TESTS

Let's face it: Some jobs involve more blood than others. A cell phone designer never interacts with blood at work, while veterinarians work with blood every day. Here, Dr. Margee Moncure answers some blood questions.

What does bloodwork tell you about an animal's health?

There are many tests you can do on blood. When people talk about bloodwork in a general way, they are usually talking about a chemistry panel and a CBC. There are many other specific blood tests that can help you further figure out what is wrong with a pet.

What's a CBC?

A CBC stands for complete blood count. It is simply what it sounds like: a count of the different kinds of blood cells — white, red, and platelets. The CBC also measures things like the width and color of the blood cells. This information can tell us if a pet is anemic or has an infection.

What's a chemistry panel?

A chemistry panel mostly measures how well an animal's organs are working. For instance, a pet with high glucose in his blood may have diabetes, or a pet with high BUN (blood urea nitrogen) might have a kidney problem or a stomach ulcer.

Can pets get blood transfusions?

Yes. You can use either fresh blood from another pet of the same species or blood that has been saved in the freezer. Blood is made up of cells and plasma and these parts can be saved separately in case a pet only needs one or the other.

Do animals ever faint when they see their blood?

I have had owners pass out at the sight of blood, but never the animal!

73

BLOOD TESTS

Biologists use blood tests to learn more about the health of wild animals, too. They only need a little bit of blood, and taking it does not hurt the animal.

Fewer Numbers?

To find out why there are fewer harbor seals in the Bering Sea and Aleutian Islands, biologists have taken blood samples to test for toxins and diseases.

No Worries!

Wild animals can attract tourists by the thousands. Biologists often wonder whether so many visitors cause the animals stress. To answer this question in the Galapagos, biologists took small blood samples from marine iguanas living on islands visited by tourists. They compared stress hormone levels in this blood to blood from iguanas living on islands without tourists. The tests did not show a difference in stress hormones.

When biologists test iguanas for stress hormones, they must take each blood sample within three minutes of catching an iguana. Why? If they wait longer, the biologists could be measuring the stress of being captured instead of the stress of living near tourists!

BLOOD TESTS

Pollution Problems

Biologists take blood samples from sharks (left) and turtles (below) to learn how the animals are dealing with pollution in their environments. After testing and measuring, they are released. Sometimes, biologists tag animals with transmitters, too.

WILD & WACKY

Stinky Blood

If you've ever squashed a stinkbug, you probably learned the hard way how they earned their common name. Stinkbugs have more than bad-smelling chemicals in their blood, though. They reflex bleed to move pheromones that talk to other stinkbugs, telling them where to find good food. Biologists may be able to use these pheromones to make traps for people's homes.

Headless Roaches?

Headless roaches may sound like fiction, but they're real. When a roach loses its head, its blood clots the wound. Because roaches have open circulatory systems, their blood isn't under as much pressure as animals with closed systems. Insects get oxygen through small holes in their exoskeleton so they do not need a nose or mouth to breathe.

Bloodsicles

How yummy is a frozen treat on a hot summer day? Many zoos make summer snacks for their carnivores by freezing blood. The blood in this leopard's snack was frozen in a plastic mold shaped like a human brain!

WILD & WACKY

Fighting Blood

When penguins fight for mates, they use their wing bones like clubs to hit each other. Fights can be bloody. When monitor lizards fight for territories, they often scratch each other with sharp claws.

Camouflaging Veins

Ever wonder how some insects can look so much like leaves? It's not just their green or brown colors that help them blend in. The veins in their wings camouflage them well with leaf veins.

Fake Blood

Hippopotamuses release reddish-brown mucus called blood sweat to keep their skin cool. Chemicals in the mucus work like sunscreen to protect hippos from the sun. Blood sweat also protects hippos from bacteria.

WILD & WACKY

Study Me!

The axolotl salamander's big eyes and fluffy gills make it fun to look at. These salamanders spend their lives under water, and they never change into adult forms, the way other salamanders do. Their gills are bright red because they are filled with oxygen-rich blood. Scientists study this animal because of its amazing self-healing ability. Axolotls can regrow their hearts, spinal cords, legs, and parts of their brains!

GLOSSARY

BLOOD: A tissue in many animals that carries oxygen and other nutrients throughout the body and removes wastes

BLOOD VESSELS: Tubes that move blood through animal bodies; includes veins, arteries, and capillaries

CELL: The smallest unit of life. Multicellular animals may have millions or even trillions of specialized cells.

HEMATOPHAGY: The feeding of animals on blood

HEMOCYANIN: A copper-based molecule that carries oxygen and carbon dioxide in many animals

HEMOGLOBIN: An iron-based molecule that carries oxygen in arthropods and molluscs; a few animals also have hemoglobin.

HEMOLYMPH: The circulatory fluid in arthropods and molluscs that contains both blood and lymph fluids

HEMOTOXINS: Toxins that affect or destroy blood cells

HIBERNATION: The time an animal spends dormant during winter months, when food is often in short supply

PLASMA: The liquid part of blood

PROTEIN: A large molecule made from amino acids; some proteins are enzymes that speed up reaction rates

TOXIN: A compound that can cause illness or damage

ACKNOWLEDGMENTS

Information from the following individuals, places, and organizations contributed greatly to this book: Adriano Aguzzi, Amateur Entomologists' Society, American Heart Association, American Museum of Natural History, Matt Anderson, Christian Arnold, Jill E. Arnold, Jon C. Aster, Christián Atala, Christopher Austin, John P. Babiarz, Ludo Badlangana, Bonnie A. Bain, Rodrigo Egydio Barreto, George A. Bartholomew, P. W. Bateman, Daniel E. Bauer, J. J. Becnel, Barbara Beltz, Ernest F. Benfield, Bioweb/University of Wisconsin-La Crosse, A. J. Blaylock, J. D. Bobb, Biology Boom, C. A. Bost, Drion Boucias, Catherine Brahic, Paul M. Brakefield, Ron Broglio, Danit Brown, Tanya Brunner, Sandra D. Buckner, Howard Franklin Bunn, Mauricio Canals, Tim Caro, James E. Carrel, Hamanda B. Cavalheri, Centers for Disease Control, Y. Chamba, J. B. Charrassin, Crystal Cockman, Cornell University College of Veterinary Medicine, Daniel P. Costa, B. Coughlin, Eugene C. Crawford, Jr., C. P. da Costa, Anne Innis Dagg, Helton Carlos Delicio, Department of the Environment and Energy/Australian Antarctic Division, Charles D. Derby, DesertUSA, Hannah diCicco, D. P. F. Duarte, Thomas Eisner, Vanessa O. Ezenwa, Jennifer Faddis, F. Fish, Kevin Fitzgerald, P.A. Fleming, Timothy Forrest, Fossil Rim Wildlife Center, J. Howard Frank, The Franklin Institute, Friedrich-Alexander-Universität, Marilia P. Gaiarsa, Kate Gammon, Ri-Li Ge, James N. George, Percília Cardoso Giaquinto, Michael A. Goetz, Helena Goscilo, Fredric R. Govedich, Carolyn Gramling, Great Lakes Fishery Commission, Bruno Grossi, Murilo Guimaraes, Shelley C. Halach, Shannon Hall, Jen Hamel, George Hammond, Y. Handrich, Ben Harder, Harvard Medical School, Mirian M. Hay-Roe, James Edward Heath, R. D. Heathcote, Anne Marie Helmenstine, R. Hibst, David E. Hill, Kirsten N. Hines, D. Hoban, Lorenz Hunziker, José Iriarte-Díaz, John B. Iverson, Donald C. Jackson, Robert R. Jackson, Howard E. Johnson, D. Jones, Sam Jorgensen, Julia C. Jones, Michiya Kamio, A. Kato, K. Kerst, Ashot Khrimian, A. Kienle, Ronald E. Kinnunen, Charles R. Knapp, Walter D. Koenig, Barbara Konig, Brenda Larison, Matthias Laska, Robert C. Lasiewski, Christine R. Lattin, Leeches Medicinalis, L. Lilge, Harvey B. Lillywhite, Y. Le Maho, Haude Levesque, L. Lilge, Harvey B. Lillywhite, Heather Sealy Lineberry, Y. Ling, D. Lutz, Alexis C. Madrigal, Ivan Maggini, Paul Manger, Payton Manning, Marine Mammal Center, Ruben Marrero, Kim Marshall-Tilas, M. Marshall, Larry D. Martin, J. R. Mason, Alan G. McElligott, Jerrold Meinwald, Amanda Melin, Joe Mello, Dini M. Miller, Jacqueline Miller, Missouri Department of Conservation, Caio Akira Miyai, Russell F. Mizell, III, Richard Mooi, P. Morrison, Caroline Müller, Y. Naito, Virginia L. Naples, National Association of Rescue Divers, National Oceanic and Atmospheric Administration, National Park Service, New York State Department of Environmental Conservation, Ximena J. Nelson, Y. Niizuma, J. Nott, Charles L. Nunn, Michael Oellermann, Patrick O'Gara, Benjamin P. Oldroyd, M. S. Patterson, David T. Peck, Caro Perez-Heydrich, Petre Petrov, Purdue University Medical Entomology, Ma Qi-sheng, Ga Qing, L. Michael Romero, Chang Rong, A. Roomer, Paul Rose, M. Rosenmann, Johan Ruud, Fabio Henrique Carretero Sanches, Sankalp India Foundation, Farzana Sathar, Katsufumi Sato, Megan Scudellari, Thomas D. Seeley, R. S. Seymour, Shkelzen Shabani, Alexandra Shapiro, W. C. Sherbrooke, E. M. Silva, Scott R. Smedley, Michael L. Smith, David L. Stachura, Stanford University/Environmental Science Investigation, R. Steiner, Karla A. Stevens, J. Stevenson-Hamilton, Mark A. Suckow, Wanda Taylor, Javier Torres, Orlando J. Torres, David Traver, Tom Turpin, Zachary Velcoff, I. A. Vitkin, Gilson Luiz Volpato, Larisa Vredevoe, Amy Wagers, Y. Watanuki, Thayer Watkins, Don Weber, Nick Wegner, B. C. Wilson, Ronald P. Wilson, Wisconsin Department of Natural Resources, C. X. Wu, Lu Dian-Xiang, Ma Yan, Liu Yin, Ed Yong, Trevor T. Zachariah, Jennifer Zaspel, H. Zhang, Bai Zhen-Zhong, Yang Ying-Zhong, Caihong Zhu, Olivia Walton Ziegler, and Leonard Zon.

Gratitude is also extended to the following photographers and photographic sources for their creative contributions: Denis Anderson/CSIRO Australia (page 75-bottom right), Leanne & David Atkinson (page 70-bottom left), Christopher Austin (page 13-top left), California Academy of Sciences/ Gerald and Buff Corsi/Creative Commons (page 65-middle left), CDC/Harvard University (page 73-top right), CDC/Sickle Cell Foundation of Georgia/Jackie George, Charles River Microbial Solutions (pages 6 bottom-right and 29-bottom), CSIRO/Australia (page 75-top right), Bruce Dale/National Geographic/Getty Images (pages 6-top and 63-top), Michelle Dang/Zon Lab/Harvard University (page 63-middle), Desmodus/Wickimedia Commons (page 66-middle), Dumi/Wikimedia Commons (page 65-bottom), Bernard Dupont/Wikimedia Commons (page 64-bottom), Steve Garvie/Wickimedia Commons (page 68-middle), Jim Gathany/CDC (pages 5-top and 72), Elegua/Shutterstock.com Elliott J. Hagedorn/Zon Lab/Stem Cell Program/Boston Children's Hospital/Harvard Medical School (page 63-top, bottom left, and bottom right), Mark Jones/Roving Tortoise Photos/Oxford Scientific/Getty Images (page 65-bottom right), Lakeview Images/Shutterstock.com, Joe Mello/NEFSC/NOAA (page 29-left), NASA (page 33-middle left, middle right, bottom left, and bottom right), NOAA Corps (page 29-top and bottom right), NOAA Ship DAVID STARR JORDAN Collection Commander John Herring, NOAA/Southwest Fisheries Science Center (page 44), Philiadelphia Zoo/Robertsphotos1/Flickr (page 66-top), Marlin Rice (page 51-bottom right), San Diego Zoo/Minden Pictures (page 76-bottom), Sandstein/Wikimedia Commons (page 67-bottom), Beverly Sinclair (page 72-bottom left), Javier Torres (page 57-top), Túrelio/Wikimedia Commons (page 73-top left), and Alan R. Walker/Wikimedia Commons (page 74-top left).

Appreciation is also extended to Beverly McBrayer (Library Media Program Director) and students at Hall Fletcher Elementary School in Asheville, North Carolina for their valuable editorial feedback.

INDEX

READ MORE, DO MORE

HAVE FUN READING: *Human Body!* by DK; *The Book of Blood: From Legends and Leeches to Vampires and Veins* by HP Newquist; and *The Blood-Hungry Spleen and Other Poems About Our Parts* by Allan Wolf

HAVE FUN WATCHING YOUR BLOOD VESSELS: Sit at a table and place one hand flat on the table's surface. After five minutes, look at the veins on top of your hand and ask a friend to measure the width of the veins you can see in millimeters. Stand up for five minutes with the same hand down by your side. Look at the veins and measure their width again. Now hold your hand over your head, high in the air, for five minutes. Look and measure again. How much do your veins change as they have more or less blood in them?

HAVE FUN SEEING WHITE BLOOD CELLS: Look up at a blue sky (but not at the sun) and you may see small specks moving across your eye. These specs are white blood cells. Why can't you see the red blood cells traveling with your white blood cells? Because light travels well through white blood cells, allowing you to see them.

The End!